‘OHANA TIME!

31 Daily Devotionals for the Hawaiian Heart

By Kahu Brian & Karen Welsh

Illustrated by Laurie Connable

Foreword by Papa Makua Wendell Davis

‘Ohana Time!

Dedication:

We humbly dedicate this book to our six grandchildren ~ Noah, Alexa, Zackson, Walter, Atlas, and Jameson. We give all the glory to God who inspired us through our grandchildren to get families back into daily Bible devotions. The book would not have been possible without the whimsical illustrations of talented Hilo artist Laurie Connable! Be on the lookout for little friends in every picture! She dedicates her drawings to her grandchildren Lily, Kade, and Aven.

Purpose:

It is our desire to encourage families to restore the Hawaiian Christian tradition of *‘ohana* devotions. Many Hawaiian families have fond memories of a family leader (Mother/Father/*Tūtū/Tūtū Kane*) gathering everyone together after dinner to lead in Christian songs, clean up any hurt feelings among the children and adults through *ho‘oponopono*, give a devotional focus from the Bible, share memory verses, and pray for each other. This daily spiritual practice will draw the generations together centered on God's Word.

Suggested Uses:

- Find a regular time that works for your ‘ohana routine
- Discuss the Hawaiian word and how the picture reveals its meaning
- Read the devotion and add your personal thoughts to it
- Practice the daily memory verse together
- Sing songs in Hawaiian and English that go with the main theme
- Remember to order and use the matching **‘Ohana Time! Coloring Book** to reinforce the themes and verses!

FOREWORD

The family or *'ohana* was important to the Hawaiian people. It still is today.

I always looked up to my grandparents (kūpuna). They shaped my life both physically and spiritually in the days of my youth and took the time each day to pour their Godly wisdom into me through life lessons, reflections, and personal experiences. Those are the days I will always cherish and hold dear. The spiritual framework of their home along with the roles and responsibilities within the hale were well-defined and understood. The authority of my grandfather "Papa," as the "*Luna o ka 'Ohana*" (Head of the Family) was clearly recognized, respected, and obeyed. My grandmother, "Mama," was a pivotal person in my life too. Every success on my resume of life points to Ke Akua (God) as lived out through *them*. They brought the Hawaiian values of the Christian faith into our family circle and at the dinner table. As a result, I could clearly see my faith through culture and culture through faith.

Under Papa and Mama's charge, every family member had an important role to help without being asked because it was true *kokua* (help) and *hana pono* (right behavior). Maintaining and establishing maluhia (peace) and lōkahi (harmony) were insisted upon, as well as rules of personal conduct that were clearly outlined and initiated. These included the importance of 'ohana (family). *hanohano (honor)*, and to never bring *hilahila* (shame) as the Hawaiian Proverb says, "*Kū i ka welo*," meaning "Whether good or bad, one's behavior is judged by the family he or she belongs to."

In my formative years, I was taught to never be rude or quarrelsome, selfish, or boastful; never to hate, but love. *"Aloha ke kahi i ke kahi,"* to always love one another, forgive one another, serve one another, admonish one another, encourage one another, honor one another, unite with one another, welcome one another, and even restore one another. "One another-ing" was the life value that paved my way to adulthood, and it began in that simple, humble, and small beginnings of my grandparent's home. I was taught to understand that wealth is not based on what you want, but what you have. Papa would say, "When you have a roof over your head, food on the table, a bed to sleep on, and love in the home, what more do you need?" I have passed these same prophetic and life-giving words on to my own keiki (children) and *mo'opuna* (grandchildren). The home is always a place of love because "God is love" (*"Aloha Ke Akua"* - 1 John 4:8). Aloha is the key to Heaven, and paulele (faith) unlocks the door. We continue to learn about the power of love and importance of clinging on to our faith, especially during difficult times.

The "heartstrings" of my kūpuna was the legacy and sustainability of the 'ohana and our daily connection with God. It was their hope that I would never stray from Him and the Christian values taught to me and to transfer this legacy to future generations. I was blessed to grow up as a part of God's "Royal Family." I believe with all my heart that it is the responsibility of every parent to command their household to keep the Way of the Lord and pass the "Royal" blessing of the Gospel to the next "Heirs," so they may be equipped to take their rightful place as future "Rulers" in the *"Aupuni O Ke Akua"* (Kingdom of God). This enables the transference of faith, favor, and destiny from one generation to the next by sharing the Good News with them. This can only happen if it begins within the home. That is why I am so excited about this book!

I have known the Rev. Papa Kahu Brian and his lovely wife, Mama Kahu Karen Welsh for decades, and I am blessed to embrace the publication of **"ʻOhana Time!"** This book provides an opportunity for the daily gathering of ʻohana together to learn a new Hawaiian word and, most importantly, it authentically connects us to *Ke Akua*. One word a day can be life changing for the ʻohana. The lessons and illustrations are colorful and wonderful tools for spiritual growth of every family member, whether young or old. These pages reveal the power of the Gospel and build a new foundation of family unity. Our kūpuna would say, *"O ke kahua ma mua, ma hope ke kukulu," meaning* "Build the foundation first, then the hale (home)."

This book will be transformational for you and your ʻohana. Both Rev. Papa Kahu Brian Welsh and his wife, Karen, are totally committed to God, their Christian faith, and family values. They are dedicated to blessing families, especially the keiki, whom they love with all their hearts. I have been blessed by them for years, and there is no doubt that you will be too.

Papa Makua, The Rev. Wendell B.K. Davis
Association Minister, CEO, and Spiritual Leader
Association of Hawaiian Evangelical Churches
Honolulu, Hawaii
March 2025

ALOHA

(Love)

"For God so loved the world that he gave his one and only Son that whoever believes in him shall not perish but have eternal life." ***John 3:16 (NIV)***

In the Hawaiian culture, the word "***Aloha***" can mean many things. You can be saying "Hello" or "Goodbye," but the main essence of aloha is "love." Everyone needs to be loved! One way to show aloha is to give beautiful lei. In Hawaiʻi Nei, we often give lei on birthdays, graduations, weddings, and other special occasions. What is your favorite type of lei? Do you like to wear a fragrant flower lei, a fun money lei, a braided ti leaf lei, or a simple shell lei? No matter what style, you always feel special when you receive one.

Ke Akua (God) gave us the best gift of aloha when He gave us His Son Iesū Kristo (Jesus Christ). Jesus died on the cross for our sins but rose again from the dead to give us the best gift of all…life with Him forever in Heaven! We become receivers of God's perfect aloha when we invite Jesus into our hearts. That is when God's aloha wraps around us like the warm embrace of a lei. It is never-ending and lasts for all eternity. We become His Keiki Aloha, (Beloved Children) and He fills us with love, affection, and new life!

Sing about it!

"JESUS LOVES ME"

Traditional Song/Public Domain

Jesus loves me this I know, for the Bible tells me so,
Little ones to Him belong, they are weak, but He is strong.
Refrain: Yes, Jesus loves me! Yes, Jesus loves me!
Yes, Jesus loves me! The Bible tells me so!

Hui: (ʻŌlelo Hawaiʻi) **Keiki aloha, Keiki aloha,**
Keiki aloha, Ke aloha o Iesū.

ALOHA

Paulele

(Faith)

"And without faith it is impossible to please God, because anyone who comes to Him must believe that He exists and that He rewards those who earnestly seek Him." Hebrews 11:6 (NIV)

Do you remember the first time you jumped off a rock into the ocean or into the deep end of the pool? You might have experienced fear of the unknown, but it helped to have a grown-up there you could trust and lean upon to catch you and keep you safe. That is called ***"paulele"*** in ʻōlelo Hawaiʻi, or "unwavering deep faith" in English. That gives a super boost of confidence when they say, "No worries, I'll catch you!" That means you believe what they say because they are completely trustworthy and true.

Jesus is the Prince of Peace. He said, "Peace I leave with you; My peace I give you. I do not give to you as the world gives. Do not let your hearts be troubled and do not be afraid." That means we can have full paulele in Him. We can jump freely into His arms, knowing He will catch us and never let us down. We can believe what He says 100% of the time! Sing this great hymn of faith!

"Blessed Assurance"

Pōmaikaʻi wale Iesū nō koʻu! He aka nō nei o ka nani ma ʻō! Na kona a ʻUhane i hoʻohānau hou, A lilo noʻu ke ola ma ʻō HUI: Kēia kuʻu lono, kuʻu mele nei, E hoʻonani ana i kuʻu Iesū. Kēia kuʻu lono, kuʻu mele nei, E hoʻonani ana i kuʻu Iesū.	Blessed assurance, Jesus is mine! O what a foretaste of Glory Divine! Heir of salvation, purchase of God, Born of His Spirit, washed in His blood. Refrain: This is my story, this is my song, Praising my Savior all the day long; This is my story, this is my song, Praising my Savior all the day long.

Iesū Kristo

(Jesus Christ)

"Jesus said, 'I am the Bread of Life. Whoever comes to Me will never go hungry, and whoever believes in Me will never thirst.'" John 6:35 (NIV)

Our picture shows a man with a Jesus tattoo making poi from the kalo (taro) root with a poi pounder. It is one of the local favorites in Hawaiʻi. It is like bread to the ʻohana and central to a healthy diet. It comes from pulling the kalo roots up from the loʻi wetlands, scrubbing them clean, steaming them until they are soft, then patiently grinding it into a thick paste while carefully adding water until it reaches the right consistency to eat. It is a time-consuming process, but once it is pau (finished), it is so yummy and good for those who eat it! Many people love putting their lomilomi salmon or salty pork from the imu (underground oven) into their poi! Do you like it that way? This ʻono kaukau (good food) has sustained Hawaiian families for many generations.

In the same way poi is made, "***Iesū Kristo***," (Jesus Christ) took the pounding of our hewa (sin) by dying on the cross. He became our true Bread of Life. Just as we require food every day, we need to learn more about Jesus. He feeds and satisfies our souls, much like our ʻōpū (stomach) feels after eating poi! Taking the right steps to learn more about Him is like softening a cooked taro root. It takes a lot of work, but Iesū Kristo is patient with us. He adds the living water of the Holy Spirit into our lives and keeps working with us until we are smoothed out and our hearts are "just right."

Discussion: Have you, or anyone in your ʻohana, ever planted or pounded poi? Do you like to eat it? What does it taste like to you? Can you believe how hard it is to grow kalo? Are you thankful that Jesus did all the hard work you? Talk about this with your family!

Jesus
Pray this
prayer together:
E Ke Akua,
(Dearest Lord)
Mahalo Nō,
(Our thanks to
Thee)
Mahalo iā ʻOe,
(We especially
thank Thee)
No ka meaʻai
(For the food)
Āmene (Amen)

‘Uhane Hemolele

(Holy Spirit)

"Not by might, not by power, but by My Spirit says the Lord God." ***Zechariah 4:6 (NIV)***

Do you know the story from long ago about High Chiefess Kapi‘olani? In December 1824, she walked barefoot through tangled vines, thick forests, and sharp a'a lava for almost 100 miles from Kona to the rim of Kīlauea Crater on Hawai‘i Island. Her purpose was to defy the goddess Pele at the active and raging lava pit so the Hawaiian people could be set free and would not live in fear, nor serve her anymore. Many Kānaka Maoli (Native Hawaiians) begged her to turn back along the way, but Ke Akua's "***‘Uhane Hemolele***" (Holy Spirit), gave her the strength, courage, and wisdom to do something hard. She decreed that if Pele destroyed her, then all should believe in the goddess, but if not, they needed to turn to the One True God. The determined High Chiefess was protected in a miraculous way as Ke Akua calmed the loud and roaring lava down so everyone could hear even the faintest whisper. Most of the crowd were in awe and turned away from worshipping and serving all the false gods and fully believed in Ke Akua.

This powerful historic account shows how the ‘Uhane Hemolele guides us through life. Iesū had something important for the High Chiefess to do, and He has a special purpose for you too. Maybe your task will be written in sacred texts and history books. Or you might lead a quiet life of faith, one that blesses your ‘ohana, friends, and community in a simple way. Remember that once you receive Jesus as your Lord and Savior, the ‘Uhane Hemolele will live within you and direct you along life's journey.

Discussion: What have you learned from this historic event? Do you think High Chiefess Kapi‘olani was brave? What do you think the people did after they left Kīlauea? Talk about it with your ‘ohana.

Baibala Hemolele

(Holy Bible)

"Your word is a lamp for my feet, and a light on my path."
Psalm 119:105 (NIV)

Do you have your own Bible? Can you read it by yourself yet? The little boy in our picture is happy to be in church and it looks like he is trying to pick up the ʻōlelo Hawaiʻi ***"Baibala Hemolele"*** (Holy Bible) from the back of his seat. Although he is still young, it looks like he wants to read it and understand how God's Word will help him through his life.

As he grows up, this little boy will learn the Bible is "Holy," because God inspired it and guided many good men called "Prophets" to write it. It took 1,500 years to complete this Book. God wanted us to know His story and learn to trust in Him. Just like the keiki in the picture, we need to reach for the Baibala Hemolele, open it up, and read it. There are so many exciting stories of adventure and faith! You will learn about Noah, Abraham, Rachel, Moses, Ruth, Esther, Mary, and so many others. Their examples teach us how to love and follow God in a deeper way.

The Holy Bible also tells us the Good News of Jesus Christ and how He brings us hope for the future and clear instructions on how we can be a part of His forever family. There is so much knowledge and manaʻo (wisdom) in God's Word. That is why we memorize scripture! We learn it, then hide it in our hearts so we know how to make good choices and do right in the sight of God. This is the perfect time to read the Baibala Hemolele and recite your memory verse aloud. Then, sing ***"The B-I-B-L-E"*** with your ʻohana!

The B-I-B-L-E!
Yes, that's the Baibala for me!
I stand alone on ʻŌlelo Ke Akua!
The B-I-B-L-E!

Baibala Hemolele
NA H

Hale

(House)

"Unless the Lord builds the house, the builders labor in vain."
Psalm 127:1 (NIV)

In the Hawaiian language, the word ***"hale"*** means "house." There are many types of homes in Hawaiʻi. They are built near the beach, forest, countryside, towns, and cities. Take a good look at this picture on the next page. The children are having fun playing hide and seek with each other! You can see they feel safe, happy, and protected by their ʻohana members. When Ke Akua is important to your family, He becomes the Greatest Protector of everyone in your house and cares about what happens to each of you.

The Bible says God is the Master Designer. He has a unique blueprint created for every person who has put their faith in His Son, Iesū. That makes Jesus the "Spiritual Builder" or Contractor. Then, the Holy Spirit partners with Him to fill your dwelling place with all good things. This includes love, joy, peace, patience, goodness, gentleness, faith, meekness, and self-control. Jesus and Holy Spirit make a great team! They want the spiritual hale inside of you to be a pleasant place with a sure foundation, dedicated fully and completely to God. It will be a home where you can grow closer by learning Ke Akua's Word, keeping His Commandments, singing songs of praise, and worshipping Him!

Discussion: What do you enjoy most about your home? What room do you like to play in the most? What are you grateful to have inside your home? A favorite blanket? Toys? Games? A Pet? Screens on the windows? Electricity? How about a refrigerator full of food? Tell your ʻohana what you enjoy most about living under the same roof with them and thank them for being there for you.

E Komo Mai

Mele

(Song)

"Sing to the Lord a new song. Sing praises to His name!"
Psalm 96:1 (NIV)

The Hawaiian Culture is filled with beautiful ***"mele"*** (song). It is the heart and soul of the people. ʻOhana enjoy gathering at home or church to play and sing kanikapila style. It is always a joyful occasion to share the music and singing passed down from generation to generation.

Today's memory verse says we are to sing a new mele to the Lord. Did you know that new songs are written every day by people just like you? Each mele goes straight to the heart of God. He loves it when people sing His praises!

Our picture shows a sweet auntie playing the guitar and making mele with her ʻohana. They look joyful! They might be singing "Jesus Loves Me," or "This Little Light of Mine." Ke Akua's greatest desire is for His ʻohana to declare His glory and marvel at His mighty deeds. Great is our Lord! He is worthy of our worship and mele!! Sing out with happiness to God! Show Him your smile and aloha!

Discussion: Do you like to sing? Do you play the guitar or ukulele? Do you have a favorite song at church? Do you like to make up your own mele or chants about the love and majesty of Ke Akua? Here are some rhyming words in Hawaiian to get you started!

Nani (Glory) with Lani (Heaven)
Mele (Song) with ʻUkulele (Small stringed instrument)
Mana (Power) with ʻIolana (Soar in the sky)
Mau Loa (Everlasting) with Aloha (Love)

‘Ohana

(Family)

"They replied, 'Believe in the Lord Jesus, and you will be saved, both you and your household.'" ***Acts 16:31 (NIV)***

A family in Hawaii is called an "*‘Ohana.*" They love to be together, play games and laugh with each other. They look forward to gathering each night to eat an ‘ono dinner and talk story late into the night.

One of the favorite foods served at every meal is poi. There are many ways to eat it. Some prefer it plain. Others like it combined with salty meat. Many enjoy it fried into a poi ball or baked into bread. There are family members who wait for days until bubbles ooze up in the poi to produce a strong sour flavor. ‘Ohana with a sweet tooth like tasty kulolo (pudding)!

Whatever you prefer, it is important to remember that poi does not make itself. It takes good soil, lots of water, and hard work by many hands to grow and harvest this food. There are many flooded lo‘i fields in Hawai'i where kalo plants are grown. On Hawai‘i Island, the most famous patches are found in Waipio Valley. For centuries, the Native Hawaiians living there have carefully passed down their mana‘o (wisdom) and skills to their ‘ohana members. That is so they can successfully farm in their ancient traditions and ways. They work together to plant, grow, harvest, prepare, and then re-plant a part of the root called "huli" back into the soil to grow a brand-new plant. If the ‘ohana follows the instructions of the kūpuna, that same kalo plant will continue to grow and produce food for many generations to come!

Our Bible verse reminds us that our Christian faith needs to be shared and tended from one generation to another. Replant your field today!

Activity: Look at the faces of your ‘Ohana. Each one is so beautiful! One by one, take their hand and tell them how much they mean to you. Let them know why they are special to you and to God. Then, pray for each other before giving goodnight honi ihu (Hawaiian kisses)!

Hau'oli Lā Hānau

(Happy Birthday)

"For You created my inmost being. You knit me together in my mother's womb. I praise You because I am fearfully and wonderfully made." Psalm 139:13-14 (NIV)

Today is a good day to celebrate! In our picture, the mouse is so excited that he is blowing bubbles. Look at the puppy. He is jumping for joy! Why? Because everyone loves a "***Hau'oli Lā Hānau***" (Happy Birthday). There are so many colorful decorations, balloons, presents, and delicious cake with candles at a party. A baby's first birthday is extra special. In the Hawaiian culture, it is a tradition for family and friends to gather and celebrate the little one with a big lū'au. There is always so much food, music, laughter, and fun!

Jesus feels the same way about children! He loves and cherishes them. In fact, He feels that way about everybody, whether young or old! He celebrates each unique and precious life and wants to make sure that everyone is together in His Father's Presence forever. That comes through trusting Iesū Kristo as your Lord and Savior!

Discussion: What did you do on your last birthday? Did you have a party and invite anyone? Did you celebrate at a park or the zoo? Maybe you went to the beach with family and had a cookout? Share your memories with your 'ohana! Sing "Happy Birthday" in Hawaiian!

Hau'oli Lā Hānau

Hau'oli lā hānau iā 'oe
Hau'oli lā hānau iā 'oe
Hau'oli lā hānau ia (INSERT NAME)
Hau'oli lā hānau iā 'oe!

Hauoli La Hanau
Kaikamahine
1
Bebe
Bebe

Pule

(Prayer)

"Rejoice always, pray continually, this is God's Will for you in Christ Jesus." **1 Thessalonians 5:16-18 (NIV)**

Do you "***pule***" (pray) every night before you go to bed? Our picture shows a keiki kneeling by her bed before she goes to sleep. What do you think she is talking to God about? Her family? Maybe she is asking Ke Akua for something? Pule is simply talking to God. He promises to always listen and answer our prayers.

Jesus taught the perfect pule called ***"The Lord's Prayer."*** Say it together!

E kō mākou Makua i loko o ka lani

Our Father Who art in heaven,

E Hoʻāno ʻia Kou inoa.

Hallowed be Thy name,

E hiki mai Kou aupuni,

Thy kingdom come,

E mālama ʻia Kou makemake ma ka honua nei,

Thy Will be done,

E like me ia i mālama ʻia ma ka lani lā.

On earth as it is in Heaven.

E hāʻawi mai iā mākou i kēia lā i ʻai na mākou no nēia lā,

Give us this day our daily bread,

E kala mai hoʻi iā mākou i kā mākou lawehala ʻana,

And forgive us for our trespasses,

Me mākou e kala nei i ka poʻe i lawehala i kā mākou.

As we forgive those who trespass against us.

Mai hoʻokuʻu ʻoe iā mākou i ka hoʻowalewale ʻia mai,

And lead us not into temptation,

E hoʻopakele nō naʻe iā mākou i ka ʻino.

But deliver us from evil.

No ka mea, Nou ke aupuni, a me ka mana,

For Thine is the kingdom, and the power,

A me Ka hoʻonani, ʻia a mau loa aku.

And the glory forever.

ʻĀmene. *Amen.*

Ho‘oponopono

(To Forgive)

"Be kind and compassionate to one another, forgiving each other, just as in Christ, God forgave you."

Ephesians 4:32 (NIV)

Pilikia (Problems) happen all the time, but getting angry at our ‘ohana members or friends does not make us feel good. One of the hardest things to say is, "Please forgive me." The picture shows two boys upset over a broken ukulele. While we do not know the whole story, their Papa is creating ***"ho‘oponopono"*** by bringing them together to forgive and restore their love for each other.

Ke Akua gave us the best example of ho‘oponopono when He sent His Son, Iesū Kristo to earth so we could be pardoned for our wrongdoing and make everything right with God. Now He desires us to forgive others too. Are you mad at someone or holding grudges? Take the time to forgive them, then ask Ke Akua to heal both hearts so true aloha flows through your relationship again.

In the same way, if you have made someone upset or angry, ask for forgiveness and try to never repeat what caused those hurt feelings again. It is important to start anew, so once you are pono (right) with each other, express your love and gratitude to them. This makes God happy and everyone else too!

Discussion: Are there some problems that you need to work out with a family member? Did unkind words, said in anger, make you sad? Did you shove your brother or sister when you were having an argument? Did you fight over what television program to watch? If you did something wrong or made someone cry, say "I'm sorry. If someone hurt your feelings, tell them, "I forgive you." The Bible is our guide. It says, "Don't let the sun go down on your anger." That means ho‘oponopono with each other before you go to sleep!

Seawear
Hawaii

Hewa

(Sin)

"For all have sinned and fall short of the glory of God."

Romans 3:23 (NIV)

How do you feel when you smell cookies baking? Do you like to snatch them right out of the oven and eat them while they are hot? What is your favorite type of cookie? Do you enjoy the ones with chocolate chips like in the picture? How about peanut butter or shortbread cookies? The boy looks like he really loves cookies because he is eating a lot of them! Do you see the problem though? The sign on the cookie jar says, "Do Not EAT." Oh no! He is disobeying! He is going to get in trouble!

The Baibala Hemolele tells us that when we disobey, it is called ***"Hewa,"*** or sin. It is what gets us in trouble with our parents and God. The good news is, when we are sorry for our choices, we can be forgiven. If the boy feels bad about disobeying his parents, he can say "I'm sorry," and then obey what they tell him. That will make it right!

Don't think you are the only one in the world who disobeys or does something wrong. We all make mistakes. But today's Bible Verse is very clear. It says, "For all have sinned and fall short of the glory of God." That means everyone! The Good News is that Jesus came to die on the Cross for all the wrong things we have done.

Discussion: When we ask Jesus into our hearts as Lord and Savior, we are saved because we trust and believe in Him. How does it make you feel to know that you are loved and forgiven even when you disobey or make bad choices? Do you feel happy? Peaceful? Joyful? Is it a relief to know you can smile and rest in Him? Talk openly with your family about it!

Tokyo
New York
Hilo
Las Vegas
Do Not EAT

Kalani

(Heavens)

"The heavens declare the glory of God; the skies proclaim the work of his hands."* *Psalm 19:1 (NIV)

Have you ever been to the top of Mauna Kea at night? There are so many stars to see! The Milky Way Galaxy is so radiant and looks close enough to touch! If your ʻohana goes holo holo (go out for a drive) near the top of a mountain or near the shoreline, if the night is clear, ask the driver to safely park and turn off the headlights. Then look up into the sky! That is when you will get the best view of ***"Kalani."*** The universe is so big compared to the earth! Do not forget to take a thermos of hot chocolate, healthy snacks, and blankets along for your adventure!

The Bible says Ke Akua made all the stars and put them in their places. Because He made everything in the heavens and on earth, we can trust Him with our lives. He shines over us, just like all those beautiful twinkling lights in the sky!

Discussion: How big do you think God is? Close your eyes and try to picture Ke Akua. He is much bigger and more powerful than we could ever imagine! Even though the Universe is big, God cares deeply about you, your ʻohana, and everyone in the entire world. He's got you safely in His Hands!! Sing about it!

He's Got the Whole World in His Hands

He's got the precious little baby in His hands. He's got mommy and daddy in His Hands.
He's got brother and sister in His Hands. He's got the whole world in His Hands!

Hui: He's got the Whole World in His Hands (X4)

He's got tūtū and papa in His Hands. He's got auntie and uncle in His Hands.
He's got my cousins and ʻohana in His Hands. He's got the whole world in His Hands!
(Hui)

Mālama

(Take Care of)

"Therefore encourage one another and build each other up, just as in fact you are doing."*   *1 Thessalonians 5:11 (NIV)

Do you like making lei? Have you ever strung a plumeria lei? It can be done quickly if lots of people help. You need to pick fresh fragrant blossoms off the trees and then string them together. The three sisters are very happy in the picture as they make a special lei. They are having such a fun time together that the lei is getting too long and is wrapping around them. I bet there is a wonderful smell where they are working. Even our mouse friend wants to help!

Our Hawaiian word today is ***"mālama."*** It means to take care, tend, protect, nurture, or serve each other. The Bible reminds us that helping others is how Jesus taught us how to live. Jesus gave us the Golden Rule in Luke 6;31, "Do to others what you would have them do to you (NIV)." It would be wonderful if we were always kind to each other! Who can you mālama today? When you are pau, don't forget to say "Mālama Pono," which means you are blessing others to live carefully and righteously with the help of Ke Akua, because He is the one who helps to show us the way!

Mālama I Ka Āina

By Leon and Malia Siu

Used by Permission

Mālama i ka ʻāina, e aloha ē	*Take care of the land, full of love*
Mālama i ke kai, e aloha ē	*Take care of the sea, full of love*
Mālama i ka poʻe, e aloha ē	*Take care of one's people, full of love*
I kekahi, i kekahi, e aloha ē	*Love one another, Love one another*

Malama
Malama
Malama

ʻĀina

(Land)

"The earth is the Lord's and everything in it; the world and all who live in it." ***Psalm 24:1 (NIV)***

Do you see the mama ʻIʻiwi (Honeycreeper) in the picture? She is feeding her keiki. She is nurturing them from the "***ʻāina***" (land). Have you ever seen a red honeycreeper in the forest in Hawaiʻi? They are so beautiful, but these birds are becoming a rare sight to see. Many animals and plants are becoming endangered in Hawaiʻi Nei. Hawaiians have an intimate and longstanding connection with the ʻāina and feel it is important to mālama for future generations because they know it provides food and nourishment for those who dwell on the island!

The Bible tells us that the Lord gave us the earth and everything in it. That means we are blessed with this beautiful place called Hawaiʻi to protect it for future generations! Have you seen God through nature? Perhaps a beautiful sunrise or sunset, a colorful rainbow, or a majestic wave breaking on the shoreline. Think about how the ʻāina inspires you and share your thoughts and memories with your ʻohana. Discuss how God wants you to "aloha ʻāina" (use loving stewardship) of the land and keep it pristine for many years to come.

Discussion: Do you want to bless others? Think of a project you can do with your ʻohana to help the ʻāina in a positive way. Can your family clean up trash along the road, the beach, or a nearby park? Would you enjoy planting a variety of native flowers or fruit trees? Think big, act locally, and see the results of your work.

Ikaika

(Strong)

"Finally, be strong in the Lord and in His mighty power!"
Ephesians 6:10 (NIV)

Have you ever tried climbing up a big coconut tree? It is difficult to do! These trees grow very tall, and a person must be ***"Ikaika"*** (strong) to get to the top! In Hawaiʻi, it is a skill that is often learned from dads or uncles, It is important because in Hawaiʻi coconuts are a source of food and milk. Our friend in the picture is happy to learn a new skill and get coconuts for his ʻohana! He is brave to climb up the tree!

Today's Bible verse tells us to "be strong in the Lord and His mighty power." Knowing Jesus makes our hearts ikaika when we love Him! This requires personal discipline in our lives by reading the Bailbala Hemolele every day and memorizing it too. Also, you should pray every day to fill your heart with God's supernatural power! You will climb to new heights of glory as you learn to draw closer to Ke Akua and grow stronger every day! Sing the song below!

"How Great Thou Art!"

E Ke Akua nani kamahaʻo, (Oh Lord my God, When I in awesome wonder)
Nāu nō i hana ka honua nei, (Consider all he worlds Thy Hands have made)
Me nā hōkū, ka uila, ka hekili, (I see the stars, I hear the rolling thunder)
Hōʻike ana i Kou mana ē. (Thy power throughout the Universe displayed)

E mele au, i Ka Hoʻōla ē, (Then sings my soul, my Savior God to Thee)
He Nani Nō, He Nani Nō. (How Great Thou Art, How Great Thou Art)
E mele au, i Ka Hoʻōla ē, (Then sings my soul, my Savior God to Thee)
He Nani Nō, He Nani Nō. (How Great Thou Art, How Great Thou Art)

Pono

(Be Righteous)

"He has shown you, O mortal, what is good. And what does the Lord require of you? To act justly and to love mercy and to walk humbly with your God." Micah 6:8 (NIV)

Has anyone ever bullied you or treated you badly? What did you do? Were you mean back to them or were you able to forgive them? Our picture shows Queen Liliʻuokalani, the last sovereign monarch of the Hawaiian Kingdom. She officially ruled from 1891 to 1893, the year when the kingdom was taken away during an illegal overthrow. The injustice of the situation was a great upset to the queen and her subjects. But she did a Godly thing when she decided to forgive all the people who were mean to her. While imprisoned in ʻIolani Palace in Honolulu, she wrote a famous song entitled "The Queen's Prayer," which focused on trusting God for justice and forgiving those who treated her badly.

She was a very ***"pono"*** (righteous) Queen because she did what was right and pleasing in God's eyes! She taught us that even when people do bad things, we can choose to be pono, to forgive, and walk in Ke Akua's Righteous Way.

Here are the lyrics for you to read or sing:

THE QUEEN'S PRAYER

(written by Queen Liliʻuokalani while under house arrest)

O Kou aloha nō (Your loving mercy)
Aia i ka Lani, (Is as High as Heaven)
A ʻo Kou ʻOiāʻiʻo, (And Your truth)
E hemolele hoʻi. (So Perfect)
Koʻu noho mihi ʻana, (I live in sorrow)
A paʻahao ʻia. (Imprisoned)
ʻO ʻoe kuʻu lama. (You are my light)
Kou nani, koʻu koʻo, (Your glory, my support)

Mai nānā ʻino ʻino, (Behold not with ill will)
Nā hewa o kānaka, (The sins of man)
Akā e huikala, (But forgive)
A maʻemaʻe nō. (And cleanse)
Nō Laila, e ka haku, (So Lord, protect us)
Ma lalo o Kou ʻeheu, (Beneath Your wings)
O ko mākou maluhia, (Let Peace be our portion)
A mau aku nō (Now and forever more)

ʻĀmene (Amen)

HOLY BIBLE

Hauʻoli

(Happy)

"...for the joy of the Lord is your strength!"

Nehemiah 8:10 (NIV)

Do you like to play in the ocean? What is your favorite thing to do there? Do you walk in the tide pools and look for little sea creatures? Do you know how to throw a net or use a pole to fish? Do you like to surf? The man riding the surfboard in our picture is ***"hauʻoli"*** (happy)! He caught a big wave and is riding it all the way to shore. Have you ever done that?

God gave us a wonderful place to live, and He wants us to be happy and enjoy it! This beautiful place called Hawaiʻi should fill you with joy from the Lord. Even when you are sad, you can remember all of Ke Akua's promises to you. God said He will always love, protect, nurture, surround, and bless you. He is the giver of all good and perfect things. Knowing how much He cares about you can make you happy and bring you joy. The Bible says we can smile at our future, because God is with us each step of the way.

Discussion: What are some of your favorite memories? Take a few moments with your ʻohana and tell them your happy memory. Make it so big and funny that everyone will laugh! Then sing the song below.

"***<u>I've Got the Joy, Joy, Joy, Joy Down in My Heart</u>***"

I've got the joy, joy, joy, joy down in my heart (Where?)
Down in my heart (Where?)
Down in my heart
I've got the joy, joy, joy, joy down in my heart (Where?)
Down in my heart to stay!

Cheeehoooooooooo!
oink oink!

Lōkahi

(Unity)

"How good and pleasant it is when God's people live together in unity!" ***Psalm 133:1 (NIV)***

Lōkahi" is the ʻōlelo Hawaiʻi that unifies and binds us all together in the greatest sense of aloha. Look at the picture and notice how carefully the auntie is weaving the lauhala. She is busy making many useful items like mats, fans, and hats that are popular to use.

Just like the lauhala, God weaves our lives together in perfect unity if we trust in Him. From the youngest keiki to the oldest kūpuna, everyone plays an important and vital role in creating and keeping unity, whether at home, work, play, church, or school. We need each other because our lives are woven together to make one connected and unbreakable ʻohana! And the good thing is, once we are entwined together, we are unified and very durable, just like the lauhala. That makes for lasting friendships and close-knit ʻohana times!

Activity: Gather a spool of sewing thread and a safe pair of scissors, then have your ʻohana gather around for this activity. Then, follow the instructions listed below.

1. Have a trusted adult tie one strand of thread around your wrist.
2. Try and break it. What happened?
3. Have the same adult tie three strands around your wrist.
4. Try and break it. What happened?
5. Follow up question: Was it stronger with three?
6. Now imagine if it was braided together like the lauhala.
7. Talk story about what you have learned with your ʻohana and friends.

Kahu

(Shepherd/Pastor)

"The Lord is my Shepherd, I lack nothing. He makes me lie down in green pastures; He leads me beside quiet waters."
Psalm 23:1,2 (NIV)

The Bible tells us that Jesus Christ is the Good Shepherd. Once you repent of your hewa and ask Jesus into your heart, you become a part of Ke Akua's flock, and Jesus leads and guides you to green pastures. That means abundance! We can trust Him to guide and protect us every day! Jesus will cover us with His love and fill us with His blessings!

Ke Akua also provides ***"Kahu"*** (Shepherd/Pastor) to watch over His earthly flock. These men and women guide and protect those in their care. It is not like a regular "job," but rather, a specific "calling from God" to set aside their life's ambitions and serve at a specific church.

The Hawaiian churches always had the greatest respect for their Kahu. In fact, the original Church Manual on Procedure, called the "*Buke Lawelima*," states: ***"The Kahu office is first in the church. The Kahu shall be to the people their leader and guide in all things spiritual and shall be honored by the congregation at all times."*** Kahu take this commitment seriously! They preach the Sunday sermon and serve at weddings and funerals. Throughout the week, they attend important meetings, events, provide blessings, and visit people at home or in the hospital to encourage them. Sometimes they even lead worship and sing!

Our picture shows a Kahu who is dressed up. He is using a calabash (bowl), filled with Hawaiian sea salt and wai (water) to give a house blessing. The Kahu prays, then he dips fresh cut ti leaves into the koa bowl and lifts them in the air before sprinkling the water around the hale. This is to show how God desires to shower the ʻohana with His blessings and protect their home!

Discussion: God is still calling people, young and old, to become Kahu! Have you ever heard God speak to you? What did He say to you? Talk to your ʻohana about it!

Hale Pule

(House of Prayer)

"...not giving up meeting together, as some are in the habit of doing, but encouraging one another—and even more as you see the Day approaching." Hebrews 10:25 (NIV)

The picture for today is historic Haili Church in Hilo Town, the oldest "***Hale Pule***" (House of Prayer) on the East Side of Hawaiʻi Island. It is famous for the thousands of Hawaiians who joined in the "Great Awakening" of the Christian faith in Hawaiʻi almost 200 years ago. It was the largest church in the world back in the 1800s. It was a time when God touched the hearts and lives of so many Hawaiians with the love of Jesus! Each weekend, thousands of people, some from far away, walked to this church in Hilo Town because they wanted to learn more about the Good News! They stayed several days at a time, sleeping in the sand or under coconut trees along the Bayfront. They brought whatever food they had to share and cooked it together. They would laugh, hug, rejoice, pray, encourage, and cry with everyone who was excited about following God.

Soon churches sprang up all over Hawai'i Nei and quickly became the heart of each community. ʻOhana of all ages attended Sunday School and services. They would bring good food to share at a "Pot Blessing," and they would eat together before splitting off to other meetings, such as Christian Endeavor Leadership Training, and rehearsals for adult and junior choirs. In the late afternoon, they would come together again to enjoy sports and games before evening services.

It is wonderful to know there are still Hale Pule in every community. They may not look the same as the one in our picture. Some congregations meet in modern buildings, warehouses, or at the beach, while others attend traditional churches. Jesus promises that wherever two or more believers are, there He is in their midst. Wherever you go, it should be a place of great importance in your life. Make it a top priority to get up and attend each week. You can learn about Ke Akua and His deep aloha for you, develop lasting friendships, and experience fun activities.

HAILI CHURCH

Paukū

(Bible Verses)

"I have hidden Your Word in my heart that I might not sin against You." ***Psalm 119:11 (NIV)***

What book is tūtū holding? Is it the Baibala Hemolele? Do you remember in an earlier devotion that studying God's Word is an important thing for ʻohana to do together? Look at the picture! It is so interesting that kitty wants to learn too! Hawaiian families used to read the Bible every day and share the ***"paukū"*** (memory verse) they learned with one another. The easiest one to say was, "Aloha Ke Akua" (God is love) from 1 John 4:8. The keiki always raised their hand and called first by their kūpuna so they could recite this verse to the others!

Our paukū today is from the Psalm of David, a great and mighty King in Israel. It tells us that having the Bible hidden in our hearts makes Ke Akua happy and it also helps us learn how to obey Him.

Encourage your ʻohana to read the Bible every day and memorize all the key scriptures. These will help everyone live for Iesū and make good choices along the way as Ke Akua brings His Word to mind. Here is a list to help your family begin hiding God's Word in their heart so they will walk in His Way.

Here is a contest! Who will learn the most scriptures in your ʻohana? Practice with each other! Which paukū will you recite? One of them? All of them?

Genesis 1:1
John 3:16-17
Romans 3:23
Romans 6:23
1 John 1:9
Ephesians 2:8-9
Galatians 2:20

2 Corinthians 5:17
Romans 8:28
Jeremiah 29:11
Hebrews 13:8
Proverbs 3:5-6
Philippians 4:13
John 14:6

Colossians 3:23
James 4:7
1 John 4:7-8
Galatians 5:22-23
1 Thessalonians 5:18
2 Timothy 3:16-17
Romans 5:28

HOLY
BIBLE

Kuleana

(Responsibility)

"Children obey your parents in the Lord, for this is right."
Ephesians 6:1 (NIV)

The children in today's picture are smiling as they use hot, soapy water and a washcloth to clean the dirty dishes. Do you have chores that need to be done every day? Chores are regular tasks assigned to you by the grownups in your life. It could be making your bed, cleaning your room, vacuuming the floor, or feeding the animals. As you get older, you may have to drive your siblings to sports practice or shop for food at the store. Whatever is on the list for the day is considered your ***"kuleana"*** (responsibility). Even if it feels humbug and you would rather be outside playing, take your job seriously. Consider it a privilege to stop what you are doing to help your family. You will feel proud when you obey your elders.

Jesus Christ had His kuleana when His Heavenly Father sent Him to earth to save all the people in the world from their sins. It was more than a chore. It was a difficult task to complete. However, Iesū Kristo obeyed His Father's Will and died on the Cross for our hewa. This was the biggest responsibility of all time. Have you believed in Jesus? That is our kuleana too and each person must decide if they want to follow Him. If you are not sure, pray this simple prayer and invite Him into your heart today.

Aloha Ke Akua,

I know You made me, and You love me. I understand that I have disobeyed You and I have wanted to be my own boss. E kala mai ia'u (I am sorry, please forgive me). I repent of being disobedient. I know that you gave Jesus to willingly die on the cross to save me from my sins and make me your child. I believe in You with all my heart and receive Jesus as my Lord and Savior.

'Āmene

Keona
Maili
I ♥ Jesus
Poi
saimin
POKE

Ho‘apili

(Close Friends)

"You are my friends if you do what I command."

John 15:14 (NIV)

There is a special place near the waterfront in Hilo, Hawai‘i called Wailoa State Park. It is a beautiful place with famous arched foot bridges to picnic with family, celebrate birthdays, fish in the calm water, or take walks with a friend. Our picture shows two girls who are "***Ho‘apili***" (close personal friends), holding hands and walking on a path with lots of animal friends nearby. Notice that each of the animals has a friend too! Life is much more exciting when we have a best friend with us!

The Bible tells us that we are friends of God because of His Son, Jesus Christ. When we learn to obey His words and love people like He did, Iesū Kristo calls us His close personal friends too! He takes us by the hand and makes our lives exciting as He walks with us by paulele every day! Not only does Iesū walk with us, but He also talks with us and stays close beside us. We can count on Him to be there every step of the way!

‘Akahi No A Hele Pu

(Just a Closer Walk with Thee ~ Hawaiian Style)

HUI: ‘Akahi no a hele pu.
(Just a closer walk with Thee.)
E maliu mai, e Iesū.
(Come closer Jesus, is my plea.)
I kela, keia la me ‘Oe,
(Every single day with You,)
E pela no,e ku‘u Haku e.
(Stand by me, oh Lord, every day.)

Makana

(Gift)

"Children are a heritage from the Lord, offspring a reward from Him." Psalm 127:3 (NIV)

Our picture features a tūtū holding her moʻopuna (grandchild). I bet the baby makes her heart joyful and happy! You can tell she loves spending time with the baby.

The Bible says children are a ***"makana"*** (gift) from the Lord. Did you know that you are God's precious gift? He made each one of us unique, with a wonderful purpose for our life. We are all one-of-a-kind. There is no one on earth quite like you, and there never will be someone like you again. Even your fingerprints are different from everyone else in the whole wide world! Ke Akua loves us so much that He also gave us a special makana of His Son, Iesū Kristo. We need to receive Jesus' gift of salvation through repentance of our hewa and asking Him to be our Lord and Savior. That is when you become a part of His forever family! This is the greatest makana of all time! Receive it today!

Discussion: Do you enjoy spending time with your kūpuna? Do you attend church together? Do they take you to beach parks? Are you invited to go to the zoo? Do they bring you along on trips to the mall or treat you to ice cream? Do they live close by or far away? What fun things have you done with them recently?

Closing Prayer

Thank you God for my family.
Mahalo Ke Akua for giving them to me.
They are gifts from Heaven above.
Wrap them all in your care and love.
ʻĀmene

MILILANI
KALEA
MALUHIA

Imua

(Move Forward)

"Trust in the Lord with all your heart and lean not on your own understanding; in all your ways submit to Him, and He will make your paths straight." Proverbs 3:5,6 (NIV)

It is exciting to see a pod of dolphins move fast in the ocean. The strong muscles in their tails push these graceful and intelligent creatures forward. Have you seen dolphins traveling near the shoreline? They are having fun as they advance through the water together! They often jump high and spin above the water as they swim. If there are high waves, they can be seen surfing near the beach! It looks like they are having a competition!

Our Hawaiian word today is ***"imua,"*** meaning "to move forward." The Bible verse tells us to "trust in the Lord with all our hearts and lean not on our own understanding" as we go through life. Just like the dolphins playing in the surf, when a person trusts in God, they are given His strength to effectively move forward. Those who truly put their faith and confidence in Jesus become more joyful and happy. They rejoice when they let go of worries, develop Godly skills, and have fun riding the waves of life! Imua!

HAWAIʻI ALOHA

Words by Rev. Lorenzo Lyons (Makua Laiana)

E Hawaiʻi e kuʻu one hānau e, (O Hawaiʻi, land of my birth,)
Kuʻu home kulaīwi nei. (My native home.)
ʻOli nō au i nā pono lani ou,(I rejoice in the blessings of heaven.)
E Hawaiʻi, aloha e. (O Hawaiʻi, aloha.)
HUI: E hauʻoli e nā ʻopio o Hawaiʻi nei, (Happy youth of Hawaiʻi,)
ʻOli e! ʻOli e! (Rejoice! Rejoice!)
Mai nā ahe ahe makani e pā mai nei, (The gentle breezes blow,)
Mau ke aloha, nō Hawaiʻi. (Love always for Hawaiʻi.)

Kokua

(To Help)

"Come, follow me," Jesus said, "and I will send you out to fish for people." Matthew 4:19 (NIV)

Have you ever been to a hukilau? It is a time when friends and ʻohana gather to pull a large net from the ocean onto the beach to bring in the kaukau (food) for a big lūʻau celebration. The children in our picture have lots of colorful fishes in their net!

Our Hawaiian word today is **"kokua,"** meaning "to help." It takes people of all ages, including the keiki, to lend their hands to help pull the heavy net filled with many fish to the shore. Even our mouse friend is trying to kokua!

The Bible tells us that Jesus wants his family to share His love with others. He said it is like casting a huge net of aloha to catch people, instead of fish. Iesū calls us "Fishers of Men," because He desires our kokua to bring all men, women, boys, and girls to salvation through Him. The good news is that we do not have to do it alone. He gives us all the kokua we need to draw all people to Him and the safety of His shore!

Activity: Use the space below to make a list of the people you will tell about Jesus. When you are done, share the names with your ʻohana and pray for each one of them!

1. ____________________ 2. ____________________

3. ____________________ 4. ____________________

5. ____________________ 6. ____________________

Kalikimaka

(Christmas)

"Therefore, the Lord himself will give you a sign: The virgin will conceive and give birth to a Son and will call Him Immanuel."

Isaiah 7:14 (NIV)

"Kalikimaka" (Christmas) is a wonderful time of the year! Presents are wrapped under the tree and lights are twinkling from rooftops. There are parties at school and lots of special dinners with ʻohana that make great memories. Hopefully, your family goes to church and learns the real meaning of the Kalikimaka season...the story of the birth of the Son of God, Jesus. One tradition many churches observe is a Christmas Eve Candlelight Service. Some children, like the keiki in our picture, dance hula to a special Christmas carol. She is dancing to "Pō Laʻi E" (Silent Night). Others may join in too! There is so much to celebrate! The Christmas story may be acted out with Mary, Joseph, baby Iesū (Jesus), Kahuhipa (the Shepherds), and the Magi (Aliʻi). Look! Our gecko friend is climbing up the Advent Candle. Auwe! We hope his feet don't get too hot standing near the melting candle wax!

Our memory verse tells us that Jesus was no ordinary baby. He was Ke Akua's one and only Son. His Hebrew name is "Immanuel," meaning "God with us." It was a miraculous birth in that little town of Bethlehem. The Angels told the shepherds to run and see this Prince from Heaven! They rushed to see the greatest gift of all! God gave it to all of us and that is eternal life through His Son. We only need to reach out and receive this precious gift.

Discussion: Have you ever attended a Christmas Eve Candlelight Service? What Kalikimaka carol do you like to sing? What is your favorite Christmas tradition? What is the best gift you ever received? Talk about it with your family.

Po La'ie
Po Kamaha'o
Mele
Kalikimaka

Hoʻolōhe

(Listen)

"He says, 'Be still and know that I am God; I will be exalted among the nations, I will be exalted in the earth.'"

Psalm 46:10 (NIV)

If you hold a seashell to your ear, it is said you can ***"hoʻolōhe"*** (listen) to the ocean. Have you ever done that? Did you hear the ocean? The little girl in our picture is sitting very quietly at the beach so she can listen carefully. I wonder what she is hearing. What do you think?

It seems as if people today are very busy every day of the week.. Even the children run from one activity to another. School, sports, friends, and family activities can fill up all our time from when we wake up until the time we go to sleep. The Bible warns us, however, to slow down, be still, and know that He is God." Ke Akua wants us to spend time talking with and listening to Him every day. It is important to pule and hoʻolōhe to God's voice throughout each day.

Take your time. There is no need to be in a rush. Sit quietly, ponder, and meditate on God's wonderous works. Think about how much He loves you.

Here is a beautiful poem written by Auntie Laurie Connable, the Illustrator of our book!

SLOW DOWN

Take it easy. Take it slow. Let My Spirit overflow.
Trust in Me and ease your pace. Slow down. Slow down.
Fill your soul up to the brim with words of wisdom, free from sin.
Words of strength, and love, and peace. Slow down. Slow down.
Give to Me your worries now. I forgive you as I know how.
Healing Love I give to you, My child. Slow down. Slow down.

Hoʻonani

(Praise)

"Let everything that has breath praise the Lord! Praise the Lord!" ***Psalm 150:6 (NIV)***

Have you ever felt so happy that you wanted to jump and shout? Maybe you won a game with a team of friends, or you were surprised with a special gift on your birthday? What a wonderful feeling to give a shout of ***"hoʻonani"*** (praise)! Have you ever felt that way at church? Some people lift their hands high and praise loudly. They may even dance around the room! Others might prefer folding their hands together in prayer and quiet worship. Both are great ways to praise God, because from Hill all blessings flow!

The Baibala Hemolele says, "Let everything that has breath praise the Lord!" This means both showing and telling God that He is awesome, and you are honored to be His child. Jumping and shouting our praise to Him is a perfect way to tell Ke Akua that you love Him! If you want to do it now...go ahead! Dance! Cheer! Jump in the air! Lift your hands and sing ***"The Doxology!"***

Hoʻonani i ka Makua mau,
Ke Keiki me ka ʻUhane nō,
Ke Akua mau hoʻomaikaʻi pū,
Kō kēia ao kō kēlā ao.
ʻĀmene.

Praise God from whom all blessings flow,
Praise Him all creatures here below,
Praise Him above ye heavenly host,
Praise Father, Son, and Holy Ghost.
Amen.

Pau

(Finished)

"I can do all things through Him who gives me strength."
Philippians 4:13 (NIV)

Do you ever have times where you want to be ***"pau"*** (finished) with something? Life can be hard at times, but that is when we need to keep on keeping on, just like the paddlers and their little mouse friend in our picture. They put in so much effort months before the big day of the race. Each afternoon they go straight to the beach after a long day of working. They take the canoe off the rack and make sure it is seaworthy. Finally, they put it in the water and spend hours paddling in the strong currents. This isn't easy. Some days the high waves cause the canoe to "huli, make a flip." The boat can turn upside down in the rough water, tossing all the paddlers into the sea! They work hard to turn the vessel over. But they aren't done yet! They still must climb into the canoe, bail out the water, and head back to shore. They never quit. Instead, they are more determined than ever to win the upcoming race and bring home the first-place trophy!

When we finish a task in Hawaiʻi, we say it is "all pau." That means "all done." Although this is the last devotional in this book, it is akamai (smart) to remember we are never "PAU" teaching our precious ʻohana members about Ke Akua. Remind each other to "keep on keeping on." Read the Baibala Hemolele and memorize the Paukū. Then "hana hou!" (repeat) and read the book again. Make sure to gift everyone in your family with the companion ***"ʻOhana Time! Coloring Book."*** It is so much fun to color together!

It is our prayer that the meaningful tradition of ʻOhana time, as beautifully expressed by Papa Makua Wendell Davis in the foreword at the beginning of this book, will be like the huli root from the top of the kalo, replanted and treasured by every Hawaiian heart for many generations to come!

Jesus
AKUA NO KA OI

Use the QR Code below for a link to free supplemental material that goes along with each devotional!

Index of Hawaiian to English Words & Phrases

Definitions in Alphabetical Order

A

A'ā. ("Ah-ah") Jagged & sharp surface of harden basaltic lava; difficult to walk on.
Ahe ahe. ("Ah-hey ah-hey") A light, gentle breeze.
'Āina. ("Eye-nah") Land; The reciprocal relationship between the land & Hawaiian people.
'Akahi. ("Ah-kah-hee") To have just, the first time, as never happened before.
Akamai. ("Ah-kah-my") Smart, clever, intelligent.
Aloha. ("Ah-LOH-hah") Love, affection, hello, goodbye, compassion, mercy, regard, mercy.
Aloha Ke Akua. ("Ah-LOH-hah Keh AH-kuh-wah") Love and affection from God.
Aloha Ke Kahi I Ke Kahi. ("Ah-LOH-hah Keh Kah-hee Ee Keh Kah-hee") To love one another. This Hawaiian phrase describes the expectation of how people should treat 'ohana, friends, and community members with mutual love, respect, and care.
Aloha No. ("Ah-LOH-hah Noh") Expressed love, to love indeed, loving mercy.
'Āmene. ("Ah-meh-neh.") Used to express agreement; so be it, the closing of a prayer.
Aupuni. ("Ah-oo-POO-NEE") A Kingdom, government, national identity, empire, or ruler.
Aupuni O Ke Akua. ("Ah-oo-POO-NEE Oh Keh AH-koo-ah") The Realm of God.
Auwe ("Ah-oo-weh") An exclamation of wonder, surprise, or fear.

C

Calabash. ("Cal-ah-bash") A large serving bowl often made from Koa or other hardwoods.; used for communal meals or blessings. Also used a term to describe close friendships.

B

Baibala Hemolele. ("Bah-EE-bah-lah Heh-moh-leh-leh") The Holy Bible. God's Word, Many books & letters inspired and written by God's Prophets throughout the centuries.

E

E Kala Mai Ho'i Iā. ("Eh kah-lah my HOH-EE-ah") To show remorse, acknowledge wrongdoing, then follow up by addressing the person offended, respectfully coming forward, and verbally saying, "I am sorry," "Forgive me," "Excuse me," or "Pardon Me." This phrase implies the offender will turn away from the wrong behavior and never do it again.
Eheu. ("Eh-HAY-oo") Having wings, winged.

H

Ha'awi. ("Hah-ah-wee") To give, grant, allot.

Hakaka. ("Hah-kah-kah") Quarrel, fight, contention.

Hale. ("Hah-lay") House, home, dwelling place.

Hale Pule. ("Hah-lay Poo-lay") House of Prayer, sanctuary, church.

Hana Hou. ("HAH-Nah HOH") To do again, repeat, an encore.

Hana Pono. ("Hah-nah-Poh-no") To do work the right way, paying attention to detail, correctly, carefully, righteously, responsibly, and aligned with Hawaiian values.

Hānau. ("Hah-now") To birth or be born.

Hanohano. ("Hah-no-hah-no") A Hawaiian value to act with honor, integrity, & distinction in all aspects of life; pomp, splendor, glory.

Hau'oli. ("How-oh-lee") Happy, glad, joyful.

Hawai'i Nei. ("Hah-VAI-ee Nay") This beloved Hawai'i, in the sense of close affection.

Hekili. ("Heh-kee-lee") Thunder, passion.

Hele. ("HEH-leh") To walk, move.

Hemolele. ("Heh-moh-leh-leh") Perfect, faultless, flawless, holy, immaculate.

Hewa.("HEH-vah") Sin, wrongdoing, missing the mark, fault, blunder, mistakes, offenses.

Hilahila. ("Hee-lah-hee-lah") Shame, embarrassment.

Hō'ano. ("Hoh-AH-Noh") Holy, to cause to form into a definite shape.

Ho'apili. ("HOH-ah-PEE-lee") A close, trusted friend, best friend, companion.

Hō'ike ("Hoh-ee-keh") To show, exhibit, make known.

Hōkū. ("Hoh-koo") A bright star.

Holo Holo. ("Hoh-loh Hoh-loh") To go for a drive, a walk, a sail; To go out for pleasure.

Honi Ihu. ("Hoh-nee-ee-hoo") To kiss nose to nose.

Honua Nei. ("Hoh-nu-ah Nay") This beloved land or earth, and its connection to the earth.

Ho'oku'u. ("Hoh-OH-koo-oo") To forgive, release, let go of a burden, dismiss.

Ho'ōla. ("Hoh-oh-lah") To give life, revive, heal.

Ho'olōhe. ("Hoh-OH-LOH-hee") To listen, to hear, to pay attention, regard, obey.

Ho'onani. ("Ho-o-NAH-nee") To praise, glorify, exalt, honor, make beautiful, adorn.

Ho'opakele. ("Hoh-oh-PAH-keh-leh") To rescue or save someone in a difficult situation.

Ho'oponopono. ("Hoh-oh-poh-no-poh-no") Forgiveness, reconciliation, problem-solving, restoring harmony, balance, and order with others by taking responsibility for one's actions, apologizing, and showing aloha to the one offended or hurt by those actions.

Ho'owalewale. ("Hoh-oh-vah-leh-vah-leh") Trail, temptation, enticement.

Hui. ("Hoo-ee") In music meaning refrain or chorus; In life meaning a gathering, or group.

Huikala. ("Hoo-ee-kah-lah") Cleanse, purify, forgive.

Huli. ("Hoo-lee") The top portion of the kalo (taro) root that is replanted back into the soil to grow a new plant. To turn around, flip.
Hukilau. ("Hoo-kee-lau") An ancient Hawaiian fishing method involving a lot of people. rhythmically pulling in a large net full of fish, followed by a community gathering where everyone shares in cooking and eating the catch of the day.
Humbug. ("Hum-bug") Hawaiian Pidgin slang. Meaning, a hassle, annoyance, nuisance.

I

Iesū Kristo. ("Yeh-SOO KREEH-stoh") Jesus Christ, the only Son of Ke Akua (God).
ʻIʻiwi. ("Ee-EE-vee") A native and rare red bird with a long, narrow beak found in forests throughout the Hawaiʻi Islands. Honeycreeper.
Ikaika. ("Ee-KAI-ka") Strength, potency, power, sturdy, force, vigor; Having one's roots deeply embedded in Hawaiian culture.
Imu. ("Ee-moo") An underground oven where food, like kalua pig, is slowly roasted.
Imua. ("Ee-moo-ah") To move forward with persistence, progress toward a goal, be resolute and determined, to rally, express loyalty, face fears with courage and confidence.
ʻIno. ("Ee-noh") Iniquity, depravity, dishonor, bad, wicked, evil, spoiled, rotten, sinful, stormy; To insult, abuse, defame, malign, persecute, or speak evil of someone; To cause damage, injury, or harm to another person.
ʻIno ʻIno. ("Ee-noh Ee noh") Anger, ill will.
Inoa. ("Ee-NOH-ah") Name, namesake.
ʻIolana. ("Ee-oh-lah-nah") To soar into the sky, float in the air like a bird.

K

Ka Haku. ("Kah Hah-koo") The Lord, Master, Overseer, Possessor, Owner, Protector.
Kahu. ("Kah-hoo") Pastor, Guardian, Caretaker, Protector, and Steward.
Kahuhipa. ("Kah-hoo-hee-pah") Shepherd.
Kalani. ("Kah-lah-nee") Heaven, of the heavens.
Kalikimaka. ("Kah-lee-kee-mah-kah") A loan word created phonetically for the English word, "Christmas."
Kalo. ("Kah-loh") A type of taro cultivated by the Hawaiians to make poi.
Kamahaʻo. ("Kah-mah-hah-oh") Wonderful, astonishing, surprising, incomprehensible.
Kānaka. ("KAH-nah-kah") Mankind, human beings in general.
Kānaka Maoli ("KAH-nah-Kah MAH-oh-lee") Native Hawaiian People Group, an individual person with a Hawaiian bloodline.
Kanikapila. ("Kah-nee-kah-pee-lah") A hybrid of two words, "Kani," meaning sound and "Pila" meaning to play string music (usually on a guitar and/or ukulele). When "ka" is placed in the middle, it means "play sound on the instrument." An impromptu slack key jam session usually taking place at the beach, church, or any gathering of ʻohana and friends.

Kapiʻolani ("Kah-pee-oh-LAH-nee") Distinguished High Chiefess; An important member of the Hawaiian Nobility who lived on Hawaiʻi Island from 1781-1841. She became a strong and mature Christian believer after the missionaries came to the islands. She walked almost 100 miles from Kona to Kīlauea to defy Pele in 1824. With her success, she instructed onlookers to abandon the goddess and worship only Ke Akua.
Kaukau.("Kow-Kow") A Hawaii Pidgin slang word for food, meal, eating.
Ke Akua. ("Keh Ah-koo-ah") Creator God, The Highest God, The Living God.
Keiki. ("Keh-kee") Children, offspring.
Keiki Aloha. ("Keh-kee Ah-LOH-hah") Expresses warmth and affection towards a beloved child, worthy of love, lovable.
Kīlauea ("Kee-lah-oo-EH-ah") To spew; An active volcano located on Hawaiʻi Island.
Kokua. ("Koh-koo-ah") To help or assist others by providing aid, hospitality, or relief in a sacrificial way, without expecting anything in return.
Koʻo. ("Koh-oh") To support, establish, brace.
Kū I Ka Welo. ("Koo Ee Kah Vel-oh") A Hawaiian proverb meaning, "Whether good or bad, one's behavior is judged by the family he or she belongs to."
Kuahiwi. ("Kuh-ah-hee-vee") Mountain.
Kulaīwi. ("Koo-la-Ee-vee") Long residence in a place, Native land, homeland.
Kuleana. ("Koo-leh-ah-nah") Responsibility, concern, privilege, stewardship.
Kulolo. ("Koo-loh-loh") A chewy and thick pudding made with taro and coconut.
Kūpuna. ("Koo-poo-nah") Grandparents; Highly respected elders who display knowledge, experience, and a strong connection to Hawaiian culture, traditions, and heritage.

L

Lā Hānau. ("Lah HAH-nah-oo") The day of birth; to bring forth life.
Lalo. ("Lah-loh") Beneath, underneath.
Lama. ("Lah-mah") Light, lamp.
Lauhala. ("Lau-HAH-lah") The method of weaving leaves from the Hala Tree.
Lawehala.("Lah-VEY-hah-lah") Sinful, delinquent, evil, offender, transgressor.
Lei. ("Lay") A Garland or wreath of flowers, or any other type of material, which draped around the neck or head to symbolize affection. The plural of lei is lei.
Liliʻuokalani. ("Lee-lee-oo-oh-kah-lah-nee") The last sovereign monarch of the Hawaiian Kingdom, ruling from January 29, 1891, until the illegal overthrow on January 17, 1893. Her name means beautiful and glorious one of the heavens.
Loʻi. ("Loh-ee") An irrigated terrace used to raise kalo (taro).
Lōkahi. ("Loh-kah-hee") A coming together with family, friends, and community to care for each other; displaying mutual respect, unity, agreement, harmony.
Lomilomi. ("LOH-mee-LOH-mee") The process of rubbing, massaging, or kneading salt into meat to enhance its flavor; A traditional Hawaiian massage technique.
Luna Hoʻomalu. ("Loo-nah Hoh-oh-mal-oo") President or chairperson of an organization.
Luna O Ka ʻOhana. ("Loo-nah Oh Kah Oh-HAH-nah") Person with authority over the family. **Lūʻau**. ("Loo-OW") A traditional Hawaiian feast usually accompanied by music and hula.

M

Maʻe Maʻe. ("Mah-eh Mah-eh") The act of physically and morally cleansing, purifying, freeing someone from flaws and impurities.
Mahalo.("Mah-HAH-loh") Conveys thankfulness, gratitude, admiration, praise, regards.
Makana. ("Mah-KAH-nah") A gift, present, reward, award, donation, prize.
Makani. ("Mah-kah-nee"). Wind, breeze.
Makemake. ("Mah-Kay-Mah-Kay") Desire, want, like, prefer, favor.
Makua. ("Mah-koo-ah") Father, a fully mature father figure, benefactor, or provider.
Mālama. ("MAH-lah-mah") To care for, preserve; action meant to protect a way of life.
Maliu. ("Mah-lee-oo") Respectfully give attention to, heed, look upon with favor.
Maluhia. ("Mah-loo-hee-ah") Peace, calm, tranquility, safety, a quiet security, serenity.
Mana. ("Mah-nah") Supernatural or Divine Power, strength, authority.
Manaʻo. ("Mah-nah-oh") Thought, idea, consideration, plan, deep reflection, and wise.
Mau Loa Aku. ("MAW-loh-(Ah)-KOO") Constantly, continually, eternally, forever.
Mele. ("Meh-leh") Oral presentations of a song or chant.
Mihi ʻAna. ("Mee-hee Ah-nah") Sorrow, the act of apologizing or confessing; Repentance.
Moʻopuna. ("Mo-oh-poo-nah") Grandchild by birth or adopted, descendent.

N

Nānā. ("Nah-nah") To behold, look at, observe, see, notice, inspect, care, pay attention
Nani. ("Nah-nee") Beauty, glory, splendor.
Nō Laila. ("Noh Lai-lah") Therefore, for that reason, consequently.
Noho. ("Noh-hoh") To sit, dwell, live, reside, inhabit.
Nuʻuanu. ("Noo-oo-AH-noo") Chilly or cool heights; Can refer to a cliff, valley, or stream.

O

ʻOhana. ("Oh-HAH-nah") Family, whether by birth or adoption. From "ʻOha," meaning offspring or children, and "Na," to belong to. It is a core concept in Hawaiian culture that shapes daily life, traditions, and community support.
ʻOiāʻiʻo ("Oh-yah-ee-oo") Fact, truth, true; To live a life of honesty, integrity, and truth.
O Ke Kahua Ma Mua, Ma Hope Ke Kukulu. ("Oh Keh Kah-hoo-ah Mah Moo-ah, Mah Hoh-peh Kay Koo-koo-loo") A Hawaiian phrase meaning, "The foundation first, then the building:" Emphasizes the importance of laying a solid foundation before undertaking any project.
ʻŌlelo. ("OH-lay-Loh") Verbal or sign language, speech, word, statement; to speak, talk..
Oli E. ("OH-lee Eh") Rejoice, chant; the vocalization of sacred text.

ʻOno.("OH-no") Pleasing, desirous, savory, good food, delightful, enjoyable.
'Opio. ("OH-pee-OH") Youth, a juvenile person considered not fully grown or matured.
ʻŌpū.("Oh-POO") Stomach; To expand, grow, swell; to rise.

P

Paʻahao. ("Pah-ah-hah-oh") To be imprisoned.
Papa Makua. ("Pah-pah Mah-koo-ah") A respected and fully mature spiritual leader.
Pau. ("Pow") Finished or done.
Pauku. ("Pow-koo") A verse of the Bible, a small portion of scripture, the stanza of a hymn.
Paulele. ("Pow-leh-leh") To implicitly believe with unwavering faith; a deep level of confidence and trust; reliance in something or someone, especially (Ke Akua).
Pele. ("Peh-ley") The volcano goddess from Hawaiian mythology.
Pilikia. ("Pee-lee-kee-yah") Problems or trouble of any kind, whether great or small; nuisance, bother, distress, or difficulty
Poi. ("Poy") Hawaiian staple food. A nutritious starch mixture made from taro root.
Pōmaikaʻi.("Poh-MY-kah-ee") Blessed, Fortunate.
Pono. ("Poh-noh") Righteous, virtuous, balanced, equitable, respectful.
Pule. ("Poo-leh") Prayer, blessing, saying grace, talking with God.
Puʻuwai. ("Poo-oo-vai") The heart.

T

Taro. ("Tare-oh") See "Kalo."
Tūtū. ("TOO-too") A Grandmother or female elder assigned that role within the ʻohana.
Tūtū Kāne. ("TOO-Too Kah-neh") A Grandfather or male elder assigned that role within the ʻohana.

U

ʻUhane Hemolele. ("Oo-hah-neh Heh-moh-leh-leh") Holy Spirit. The One given to us by Jesus Christ to dwell inside of us and be our Helper.
Uila. ("Oo-ee-lah") Lightning or electricity.

W

Wai. ("Vai") Fresh water.

ABOUT THE AUTHORS:

Kahu Brian and Mama Kahu Karen Welsh met at Kailua High School on ʻOahu in 1976 and have been married more than 45 years. They trusted Jesus Christ as their Lord and Savior as children. They both felt God's call to serve as Pastors (Kahu) and began training at International Bible College in Nuʻuanu on Oahu and Dallas Theological Seminary. They served in several churches before they were called to Hawaiʻi Island, where Kahu Brian served at the historic Haili Congregational Church in Hilo for almost 19 years. During this time, they stepped into many leadership roles to benefit Hawaiian churches and people. Mama Kahu Karen served as the President of the Woman's Board of Missions for the Pacific Islands. While in office, she updated, wrote the epilogue, and re-published the "Memoirs of Henry Obookiah," the firsthand account of the earliest known Hawaiian Christian Convert, Henry Ōpūkahaʻia. Kahu Brian Welsh has served as the "Luna Hoʻomalu" (President of the Board) of the Association of Hawaiian Evangelical Churches (AHEC) for many years and has partnered with many Christ-centered Pacific people groups. During this time, he has built a strong spiritual connection with Papa Makua Wendell Davis, the CEO of AHEC. Their ongoing goal is to intentionally restore core Hawaiian Christian values, including a daily ʻohana time. The heart of these devotional times is learning how to unconditionally love Ke Akua and each other.

A NOTE FROM THE ILLUSTRATOR:

"Praise God from Whom all blessings flow! Mahalo Ke Akua for the gift of creativity, for my ʻohana, and my dear friends, including Kahu Brian and Karen Welsh. I have so much gratitude for the Kānaka Maoli, and aloha for everyone who live in Hawaiʻi Nei and beyond."

Made in the USA
Columbia, SC
20 April 2025

bbf99af3-b40f-461a-a754-af2119fb239eR03